Victorious Bible Curriculum

THE BEGINNING (PART 1 OF 9)

God created a home for mankind, and placed us in it to tend and guard it as His image. When we rebelled, God promised a seed of the woman to one day restore creation — and preserved that seed when our violence filled the world.

THE PATRIARCHS (PART 2 OF 9)

God chose Abraham to be the custodian of the line through which the promised redeemer would come. Abraham's grandson Jacob became the father of the twelve tribes of Israel, a nation that would bless the whole earth.

THE EXODUS (PART 3 OF 9)

For 400 years, God grew Jacob's tiny family into a nation. Through Moses, He released them from slavery to give them a new home. Despite the faithless first generation's rebellion, their children would inherit the promised land.

CONQUEST AND JUDGMENT (PART 4 OF 9)

Under Joshua, the children of the exodus conquered the promised land. After they settled in, they fell into idolatry and suffered under foreign domination. Time after time, they needed God's deliverance through a head-crushing judge.

THE KINGDOM OF ISRAEL (PART 5 OF 9)

God used Israel's first kings, the vacillating Saul and the head-crusher David, to give Israel peace. Solomon built a prosperous kingdom, which then split and fell into idolatry. After 70 years' exile in Babylon, God restored them to the land.

THE COMING OF THE MESSIAH (PART 6 OF 9)

The long wait for the serpent-crushing redeemer came to an end with the birth of Jesus of Nazareth. Raised in Galilee and baptized in the Jordan, He began to proclaim the kingdom of God and demonstrate God's love and power.

THE MINISTRY OF JESUS (PART 7 OF 9)

The blind could see, the sick were healed, the dead raised. The kingdom of God was truly at hand. But the leaders of Israel rejected the One God had sent to save them from their sins and deliver them into God's kingdom.

JESUS' FINAL DAYS (PART 8 OF 9)

On Thursday, before His arrest, Jesus ate one final meal with His disciples. Then He was arrested, beaten, falsely accused, tried, convicted and crucified. But death could not hold Him and the grave could not contain Him.

THE BEGINNING OF THE CHURCH (PART 9 OF 9)

After His resurrection, Jesus' followers received the power of the Holy Spirit to disciple the nations of the world, baptizing them and teaching them all that Jesus had said. Christ's body grew and began to crush the enemy's head under her feet.

Copyright © 2016 by Joe Anderson and Tim Nichols

All rights reserved
Printed in the United States of America
First Edition

No part of this book may be reproduced in any form or by any electronic or mechanical means, including information storage and retrieval systems, except for brief quotations in printed reviews, without the prior permission of the author.

Unless otherwise indicated, all Scripture quotations are taken from the New King James Version®. Copyright © 1982 by Thomas Nelson, Inc. Used by permission. All rights reserved.

Scripture quotations marked (NIV) are taken from the Holy Bible, New International Version®, NIV®. Copyright © 1973, 1978, 1984, 2011 by Biblica, Inc.™ Used by permission of Zondervan. All rights reserved worldwide. www.zondervan.com The "NIV" and "New International Version" are trademarks registered in the United States Patent and Trademark Office by Biblica, Inc.™

Author's translation or paraphrase indicated by an asterisk after the reference.

Illustrations by Gustave Doré
Colorized and modified by William Britton

Praise for Headwaters Bible Curriculum

These lessons are not just a way to teach the Bible to middle school kids. As I read the lessons, I found both my head and my heart irresistibly engaged. Joe and Tim have opened the grace and truth of God's Word in a way that seriously lifts us towards Christ while nudging us outward towards the world. I recommend these studies for both devotional and motivational reading!

Dave Cheadle, President of the Rocky Mountain Classis, Reformed Church of America

While I have spent quite a bit of time studying the Bible myself, I find your ideas and themes to be real food for thought and they help tie together much of the story God is telling throughout... I've already talked with people about your curriculum and have recommended they look into it for their own families. I can't loan out my copy for their perusal, because I'm using it everyday!

Linda Kidder, Home Educator, Colorado

I LOVE THIS BOOK!!!! We're just finishing up the Garden narrative. We've had such fruitful discussions—I have been pleased with it in every way. In fact, I'm hoping our church will start using it. I haven't had any problems or difficulties using the curriculum, I ONLY have good things to say about it. In fact, I'm in danger of writing in all caps I'm so enthusiastic about it.

Leah Robinson, Home Educator, Texas

I am really enjoying having this resource to work from and steer our lessons!

Christy Johnson, Bible Teacher, Bingham Academy, Ethiopia

Our family actually loves the curriculum. My children are in 5th and 8th grade and the content has suited both of their levels perfectly. To this point we hadn't found a curriculum that taught the Bible at such a detailed level that has also kept the kids engaged. We've had to slow down on the materials because otherwise they would be through them well before the school year is up. We are planning on buying the rest of the series.

Chris Turner, Home Educator, Colorado

How to Use This Book

This series of little manuals walks you through the biblical Story from end to end. Just read. Here are a few things you might want to keep in mind as you read through the Story.

- Try to love the characters. God does....
- The story is written in such a way as to make sin look stupid, but remember that the characters are all real people. No matter how stupid the choice, a real person actually looked at the options and then picked that particular one for reasons that seemed pretty good at the time. Nobody gets up in the morning and says, "I'm going to make stupid life choices that people will be mocking for centuries." Try to see it from their point of view. Ask yourself, "Why did this look like a good idea at the time?" That's how you learn to recognize temptations. It's easy to see sinful and stupid choices for what they are in hindsight, but in the moment it's often very hard. So learn to think through what these choices looked like from the inside, in the heat of the moment — you'll be amazed what you learn about yourself.
- Pay attention to the patterns. We'll point out a bunch of them as we go through the Story, but try to spot them yourself, too. If you can learn to read the Word and see the patterns in the Story, you will become able to read the world around you and see the patterns in the story God is telling right now.
- Each lesson comes with a psalm. The psalms provide us with another lens through which to look at the Story, and God has a lot to teach us that way. Sometimes we've given you an activity that will help integrate the psalm with that episode in the Story. Other times, we've just given you the psalm, and we're going to let you fill in the blanks. Read over the psalm a few times, then go into the lesson and see what comes to you. You'll be surprised what you can learn.
- As with any book that talks about Scripture, don't necessarily take our word for anything. Imagine you're sitting in a living room or around a campfire with us, and we're just talking about the Story. You're free to disagree, correct, challenge our understanding. The Word is the authority, not us — so grab your Bible and look things up yourself.

You'll find a section labeled "Activities" following the lesson. The point of this section is to immerse you as deeply in the Story as possible, through prayer, meditation on the Story, and other exercises. The "Evaluation" questions at the end of each lesson will help you to check your understanding of the material.

For Small Group Leaders
Have everyone in the group read the lesson ahead of time. Depending on how involved your group is, you can have them engage some or all of the activities, or you can save those for group time when you're together. The evaluation questions might serve as starters if the conversation lags.

For Homeschoolers
Have your student read the lesson and complete the activities. (Some might be more appropriate as whole-family activities.) You can use the evaluation questions as a quiz or as discussion starters to check your student's comprehension of the lesson.

Table of Contents

Unit 6 The Conquest ... 7
    Lesson 6.1 God Renewed His Covenant with the Second Generation ... 9
    Lesson 6.2 The Second Generation Consecrated Themselves ... 15
    Lesson 6.3 Moral Failure Impeded Conquest: Ai Routed Israel, but God Redeemed ... 23
    Lesson 6.4 The Gibeonite Deception and Israel's defeat of the Southern Amorite Alliance ... 29
    Lesson 6.5 Israel Conquered and Divided the Land ... 39

Unit 7 The Judges ... 45
    Lesson 7.1 Israel Failed to Take the Land and Fell into a Cycle of Slavery and Deliverance ... 47
    Lesson 7.2 The Head-Crushing Women of Judges ... 53
    Lesson 7.3 Samson Crushed the Philistine Heads ... 61

UNIT 6: THE CONQUEST

Since the first generation of Israel was so fixated on dying in the wilderness, God gave them their wish, allowing that generation to die over 40 years of wandering in the wilderness. Near the end of the 40 years, the second generation defeated Sihon and Og and took the land of the giants east of the Jordan. To prepare them for life in the land, Moses recounted the history of the first generation and reiterated the Law and God's covenant. Moses then died east of the Jordan, leaving Joshua as the leader. Joshua led Israel through the waters of the Jordan and into the land. There the people consecrated themselves and the men were circumcised before partaking of the Passover. God then gave Israel victory over a major stronghold in the land: Jericho's walls fell after they simply walked around the city and shouted, and they utterly destroyed the city as God had commanded.

Defeating such a strong foe made Israel overconfident, and they went after the next enemy, a small city called Ai, without seeking the Lord. Ai routed Israel, and 36 men died. When Joshua cried out to God, God explained that someone had stolen cursed plunder from Jericho. Just as God fought for Israel when they were obedient, so God would give them to their enemies when they were not. God led Joshua to Achan, who had stolen from Jericho, and he and his whole family were stoned and burned. With the sin removed from Israel, God led them back to Ai for a decisive victory, then called them to Mt. Ebal to renew the covenant.

Most of the peoples of the land united against Israel in battle, but the Gibeonites had a different strategy. They convinced Israel that they were from a far country, and without consulting the Lord, Israel made a peace treaty with them. Discovering the deception too late, the Israelite leadership confronted the Gibeonites, but still honored their treaty with them. Five other Amorite kings from the south, angry with Gibeon's treaty with Israel, attacked Gibeon. The Gibeonites called for help under the terms of the treaty, and Israel marched all night and fought the five kings all the next day. Seeing that the enemy would escape at nightfall, Joshua called on the sun to stand still, and the resulting long day provided enough time for Israel to destroy the Amorite army completely. Meanwhile, the five kings themselves were found hiding in a cave. Joshua had the mouth of the cave blocked with stones while the battle was finished; then the Israelites took the kings out of the cave, stepped on their necks and hung them on trees to die. At sunset, the bodies were thrown back into the cave and covered with stones as a memorial. With the five kings defeated, Israel took Makkedah and then campaigned through the weakened southern part of Canaan.

With Israel strong in the south, the northern Canaanites united under Jabin, king of Hazor. God promised Israel the victory, so they launched a preemptive strike against the Canaanites at the waters of Merom and defeated the combined army, then pursued them back to their cities and destroyed them. Israel then swept through central and southern Canaan, destroying the remaining giants and leaving only the Philistines in the southwest and pockets of Canaanites throughout the land. Joshua divided the land to the tribes, who went into their own allotments and took possession of the land, entering into rest.

I call **heaven and earth**
as witnesses today *against you*,
that I have set before you
life and death,
blessing and cursing;
therefore **choose life**,
that both you
and your descendants may live.

Deuteronomy 30:19

LESSON 6.1

God Renewed His Covenant with the Second Generation (Overview of Deuteronomy)

UNIT 6

THE STORY

Lesson Theme - God renewed Israel's hope with the second generation.

The first generation of Israel that came out of Egypt had seen the mighty hand of God. He had delivered them out of Egypt through the plagues and the Passover, He had miraculously parted the Red Sea and provided them food and water in the wilderness. But in spite of all of God's provisions, the people of that generation were untrusting and full of complaints. Finally, at Kadesh Barnea they rejected God's leadership into the promised land and consequently committed themselves to wandering in the wilderness for 40 years, never getting to enter into the promised land. While they were dying off in the wilderness, God renewed His covenant with their children: the second generation, who *would* get to enter into the land. "Deuteronomy" means "second law"; it is the record of the covenant with the second generation.

Deuteronomy can be outlined in three major sections. The first section recounts the history of the first generation. In the second section, Moses gave the Law to the second generation. The last section is forward-looking and tells the second generation (and following generations) how they can expect to be blessed if they keep the covenant and what they can expect to happen if they don't. You have just completed lessons on the Law and the history of the first generation, so the bulk of this lesson is focused on the forward-looking third section.

OVERVIEW

When the first generation of Israel rebelled against God's plan for them at Kadesh Barnea, God declared that they wouldn't enter the land, but rather wander in the wilderness for 40 years. Near the end of the 40 years, the people of Israel had defeated Sihon king of Heshbon and Og king of Bashan and had claimed the land to the east of the Jordan. But they weren't allowed to enter the land. Deuteronomy means "second law" and it is Moses' address to the second generation of Israel before they entered the land. In it, Moses recounted the history of the first generation, reiterated the Law to the second generation, and told them about the blessings of obedience to the covenant and curses of disobedience to the covenant.

SOURCE MATERIAL

- Deuteronomy, especially chapters 29-31
- Psalm 95
- Galatians 6:7

The first section reviews the history of the first generation. You might remember that this generation of Israelites were complainers. They complained before they left Egypt and before they crossed the Red Sea. They complained in the wilderness when they didn't have food *and* when God provided them with more than enough. Ultimately, they didn't believe that God could give them the land. As a result, all of their

Unit 6: The Conquest

OBJECTIVES

Feel...

- sadness at what the first generation had given up.
- joy that the first generation experienced some victory on the east side of the Jordan.
- excitement for the second generation to enter the promised land.
- the weight of the potential consequences (both good and bad) of the covenant.

Understand...

- the purpose of the book of Deuteronomy and what the word "Deuteronomy" means.
- what the blessings of obedience would be for Israel in the land.
- what the curses would be for Israel if they failed to keep the covenant.
- what Deuteronomy foretells about Israel's future and the hope of repentance.

Apply this understanding by...

- observing how the principle of "reaping what you sow" has played out in your own life.
- discovering areas where you are reaping what you have sown in disobedience and learning how to repent of these things.

complaints about dying in the wilderness turned out to be prophecies that came true. Before that generation had all died off, the Lord gave them victory over their enemies on the east side of the Jordan (Sihon King of Heshbon and Og king of Bashan) (Num 21:21-35). Ultimately, that generation died off before their children crossed the Jordan (except Joshua and Caleb).

The next (and the biggest) section of Deuteronomy is a second giving of the Law, this time to the new generation. It was necessary for the Law to be repeated because the first generation had rejected the blessings of the covenant, and so God made the covenant again, which included giving the Law again. There are some minor differences in the laws in Deuteronomy and the laws in Exodus since the laws in Exodus anticipated worship in a mobile tabernacle, and the laws in Deuteronomy anticipated worship in a fixed location in Israel.

For our purposes, we want to focus on the last major section of Deuteronomy which deals with the blessings and curses for covenant obedience and disobedience. As the history of Israel progressed, Deuteronomy was considered the fundamental covenant document by which the nation was held accountable. It is important to have a good grasp of the general sense of what Israel was bound by, since this will be helpful in understanding the rest of the Old Testament.

The main points in the last part of Deuteronomy
God gave Israel a list of blessings for obedience and curses for disobedience to His Law and instructions (Deut 28). The blessings were glorious: life, prosperity, health and success against their enemies. The curses were as painful as the blessing were glorious: failure of crops, expulsion from the land, death, plagues, madness and folly. This is God's covenantal version of "you will reap what you sow" (Gal 6:7). This is the way life works. If you live as God calls you to live, you will be blessed; otherwise, you will experience suffering and hardship. The same is true for you as was true for Israel back then.

But Deuteronomy goes one step beyond saying what would happen to Israel *if* they disobeyed. It actually prophecies that they *would* fail and they *would* be expelled from the land and scattered (Deut 30:1). But God is merciful; if Israel turned from the Lord, *He would not cast them off forever.* Of course He wouldn't; He had promised to Abraham many generations before that he would be a blessing and that the whole earth would be blessed through him (Gen 12:2-3). Israel's restoration was assured, but not until they repented (Deut 30:1-7). Likewise for us, if we fall into sin and turn from the Lord, we will reap what we sow... but if we turn back to Him in repentance, we will be restored!

In order to help the next generation of Israel learn and take these blessings and curses to heart, Moses prescribed an elaborate ritual for them to perform when they entered the land (Deut 27). The instructions were as follows:

- They were to write the words of the Law on stones and set them up on Mt. Ebal.
- They were to build an altar to the Lord on Mt. Ebal and offer burnt offerings.
- The tribes of Simeon, Levi, Judah, Issachar, Joseph and Benjamin were to stand on Mt. Gerizim to pronounce blessings.
- The tribes of Reuben, Gad, Asher, Zebulun, Dan and Naphtali were to stand on Mt. Ebal to pronounce curses.
- The Levites were to pronounce specific curses for people who disobeyed the Law, and the people would respond by saying "Amen."

God wanted to make sure that the people of Israel, generation after generation, would be constantly reminded of the covenant and the blessings and curses that stood before them. In keeping with this, Moses instructed the Levites to read the entire book of Deuteronomy to the people of Israel every seven years (Deut 31:11). Furthermore, the king of Israel would be required to write out a copy of the entire book for himself (Deut 17:14-20).

The book of Deuteronomy ends with Moses passing the baton of leadership to Joshua who would lead the people into the land, and finally, with Moses' death. Joshua and Caleb would be the only ones from the first generation to enter and possess the land.

APPLICATION

Deuteronomy is a covenant that rewards obedience with blessings and disciplines disobedience with curses. Whenever there are consequences spelled out in Scripture, human tendency is to focus on the negative. But the blessings spelled out in Deuteronomy were pretty awesome—lots of kids, peace in the land, plentiful crops; on and on. God is still that way—He loves to bless us, and when we walk with Him, blessing is inevitable.

Unit 6: The Conquest

ACTIVITIES

1. Journal Time: Blessings and Curses. The blessings and curses of the covenant are a high-resolution picture of what it means to reap what you sow. This principle still applies today, and we have to live with the consequences of our sins. The good news is that, just like Israel was able to repent and be restored, so can we. Write about the following.

Spend a few minutes thinking through your life and how your are reaping what you have sown. This should include both good and bad stuff. God is just as faithful to reward us for good things that we have done as He is to discipline us for bad things we have done. Write down any of your thoughts.

_____
_____
_____
_____

Write a prayer of thanks to God for the areas of your life where you have been faithful to Him and have experienced the blessings for obedience. _____
_____
_____
_____

In the areas where you have experienced or are experiencing the consequences of disobedience, write a prayer asking God to reveal anything that you still need to repent of. As He reveals these things to you, repent of them and ask God for restoration. _____
_____
_____
_____

Lesson 6.1

EVALUATION

1. What does the word "Deuteronomy" mean? _____
_____

2. Why was Deuteronomy written? _____
_____

3. What would the book of Deuteronomy mean to future generations of Israel? _____
_____

4. Summarize how Israel would be blessed if they kept the covenant. _____
_____
_____

5. Summarize how Israel would be cursed if they were disobedient to the covenant. ____
_____
_____
_____

6. What does the book of Deuteronomy indicate about Israel's future? _____
_____
_____

   Would there be any hope when this happened? _____
_____
_____

LESSON 6.2

The Second Generation Consecrated Themselves to Receive the Land in Conquest

UNIT 6

THE STORY

Lesson Theme - The second generation trusted God and prepared for conquest.

This lesson teaches that preparation is necessary for conquest and *not* sharpening swords and polishing spears, but consecration to God. The armies of Israel destroyed the walls of Jericho without a weapon, but they were operating out of a place of consecration to the Lord. Shortly before they took on Jericho, Joshua was commissioned. The people had also been baptized in the Jordan, circumcised at Gilgal, and had eaten the Passover.

Conquest in the Bible

Man was created to have dominion over the earth, but he forfeited his authority over the earth when he submitted to the serpent and ate from the fruit of the tree of the knowledge of good and evil. The first generation of Israel was called to enter the land and take dominion over it, but they, like Adam and Eve, failed to trust God and enjoy what He had promised. The second generation of Israel trusted the Lord and stepped confidently into the land, expecting Him to give it to them. The story of the conquest is the story of God *giving* Israel dominion over the land.

This lesson isn't the first time we have seen conquest in the Old Testament (Abraham conquered Chedorlaomer and therefore, inherited his conquest of the land—Gen 14); but here, in the book of Joshua, is the fullest picture of conquest until the book of Acts. But to properly understand what's going on here, we need to see what

OVERVIEW

The first generation of Israel complained and died in the wilderness. God chose Joshua to replace Moses and encouraged him not to be afraid as the second generation went into the land. Joshua passed this encouragement on to Israel and then led them miraculously across the Jordan and into the land. Once in the land, the people consecrated themselves, and the men were circumcised; then the people partook of the Passover. God then gave them possession of their first city in the land: Jericho's walls fell after they simply walked around the city and shouted.

SOURCE MATERIAL

- Joshua 1-6
- Psalm 23
- Proverbs 3:5-6

conquest means in the context of the big Story. Conquest is what it takes to gain dominion of land that has been forfeited to the enemy. Adam and Eve were given dominion of the whole earth, but they forfeited it *all* to the enemy. Therefore, in the big Story, it is necessary for the people of the King to go on conquest in *all* of the earth.

The theme of conquest lends itself to one central practical lesson. For us, mission is conquest. When Jesus told His disciples to go to the whole earth and preach the gospel, He was telling them (and us) to go on conquest: to reclaim for the gospel the ground that the enemy has taken.

Unit 6: The Conquest

OBJECTIVES

Feel...

- joy that Israel finally entered the promised land.
- awe at God's power in drying up the Jordan and in knocking down the walls of Jericho.
- gratitude that God calls us to consecrate ourselves and enjoy Him rather than simply work hard.

Understand...

- what conquest means in the big Story and what it means for us.
- why God saved Rahab and her significance in the seed-line.
- how the crossing of the Jordan, circumcision and Passover prepared Israel for conquest.
- what God had Israel do to bring down the walls of Jericho.
- that God *gave* Israel the land because they were His people; the story of the conquest is not about working hard, but receiving gifts from God.

Apply this understanding by...

- looking at your life to see if you are working to find some way to earn God's satisfaction or find your own fulfillment.
- repenting of areas where your are working for the wrong reasons and finding ways to consecrate yourself to God instead.

Our mission includes discipling people into God's kingdom, providing for the needy, and generally acting like Jesus did in the world. Our conquest (like Israel's) is a story of God *giving* us territory. Our victory was secured when Jesus crushed the head of the serpent on the cross. We work from the finished work of Christ.

Israel consecrated for conquest
Joshua 1 starts out with the commissioning of Joshua to take the place of Moses and lead Israel into the land. God encouraged Joshua to have courage and not be afraid *because* He would be with him wherever he went (Josh 1:9). Remember, *God was giving* the land to Israel; He was not telling them to go conquer it in their own strength. This contrasts with the first generation who would not trust God and lived in fear. Joshua took God's encouragement to heart and heartened Israel with the same encouragement.

The story of Rahab and the spies (Josh 2) is not central to this lesson, but there is one point you need to understand. Rahab, a Canaanite, was saved because she believed in Yahweh (see Heb 11:31 and Jas 2:25). The sparing of Rahab helps reinforce the point that God was not arbitrarily seeking the death of the Canaanites; as a nation, they really were the seed of the serpent, but not all of them. Rahab was so highly esteemed by the Lord that her name shows up in the genealogy of Jesus (Matt 1:5).

We now come to the crossing of the Jordan (Josh 3-4), which was the baptism of the second generation. This parallels the story of the first generation crossing the Red Sea. (1) The priests were told to step into the water *before* the river stopped flowing (Josh 3:13), much like God ordered the first generation to walk down toward the waters of the Red Sea before He parted them. (2) The ground of the riverbed became dry (Josh 3:17), just like the first generation crossed the Red Sea on dry land. (3) They went "under" the water of the Jordan (a baptism), just like the first generation went "under" the water of the Red Sea. (4) These events were reported to the

Amorite and Canaanite kings on the west side of the Jordan, and as a result, "their hearts melted in fear and they no longer had the courage to face the Israelites" (Josh 5:1, NIV), fulfilling the words of the song of Moses in Exodus 15:15-16, "...all the inhabitants of Canaan will melt away; fear and dread will fall on them..." The crossing of the Red Sea and the crossing of the Jordan both put the fear of God in the Canaanites.

Following the crossing of the Jordan, the army of Israel set up camp at Gilgal to prepare to go to battle against Jericho. Two important events happened while they camped there. First, God told Joshua to have all the men circumcised (Josh 5:2). The first generation of Israelites were circumcised when they left Egypt (or even as children there), but these men had all died off and had failed to circumcise their children while wandering in the wilderness (Josh 5:5). The important point here is that the circumcision of the second generation finally "rolled away the reproach of Egypt from [them]" (Josh 5:9). The first generation brought the reproach of Egypt with them into the wilderness, and it resulted in complaints, lack of trust in the Lord and disobedience to His commandments (not the least of which was to fail to circumcise their children). This circumcision at Gilgal in the promised land was, for the Israelites, the final disconnection from Egypt and identification with the land.

The second important event at Gilgal was the celebration of the Passover (Josh 5:10). The first generation apparently did not celebrate Passover in the wilderness after the second year, though they should have. But now, after crossing the Jordan, the new generation celebrated the Passover. One of the central lessons of the Passover is that God is the Deliverer; this was a lesson the Israelites needed to be reminded of as they went into battle. If they were victorious in battle, it was because God had given them victory.

Each of these events of crossing the Jordan, being circumcised, and celebrating the Passover prepared the Israelites to have the right kind of thinking about God and consecrated them to God. In the crossing of the Jordan, the people went through a death and resurrection and were set apart as God's nation (now united in Joshua). When the men were circumcised, they were separating themselves from Egypt and covenantally identifying themselves with God (see Gen 17). And when the people took the Passover, they recognized God as the Deliverer. Each of these events taught the Israelites that the conquest was an act of God, and they only received the land as they united themselves with God.

Israel defeated Jericho
Finally, the nation of Israel went after Jericho. Notice how God spoke to Joshua about taking the city: "I have given Jericho into your hand" (Josh 6:2). It was already done; the people only had to follow God to receive it. For six days, they marched around the city once a day, with the armed men before the ark of the covenant (God's presence) and the rear guard following behind (Josh 6:8-14). Jericho was a small city, only about half a mile around, so it would not have taken very long to circumnavigate. The Israelites made a lot of noise as they marched, but not with their voices, just with trumpets. On the seventh day they went around the city seven times and ended with a loud shout that brought the walls down (Josh 6:15-21). The army attacked the city and killed every person and animal inside, except Rahab and her family, as the spies had promised. God *gave* His consecrated people the city. It would have been easy for Israel to rely on their own understanding—you conquer cities with swords and bows, not with trumpets and marching, but God had a different path for them to follow (Proverbs 3:5-6).

APPLICATION

God has called us to conquest, to mission, but this is not a call to just "get to work." Rather, the call to conquest is *first* a call to consecration, feasting and rest, and then to work. The call to conquest is a call to join God in what He has already done and what He is currently doing. This implies a call to repentance in areas where we are trying to work to please God rather than giving ourselves to God so we can work. This also means that if we are not working, something has gone wrong. The application here is for you to diagnose your life to see if you are trying to earn God's satisfaction or find your own fulfillment through your labors. Of course our commission is the Great Commission (not defeating the Canaanites as Israel's was). We are called to make disciples of all nations—in a way, defeating the enemy by the power of the gospel.

ACTIVITIES

1. The Seed-Line: Important Ongoing Activity. Continue the seed-line project you started in Lesson 2.2 in *The Beginning*. Your seed-line should have a line of descendants from Adam to Abraham; continue vertically down the page from Abraham as far as you know by memory. From there, continue down to Salmon using Matthew 1. Matthew indicates that Rahab was Salmon's wife, so write her name off to the right of the center line in the genealogical line. Notice that, along with Tamar, Rahab was considered important enough to get mentioned in the line of Jesus. You can add other details off to the side if you'd like (brothers of those directly in the seed-line, for example).

2. Journal Time. Write in the space on the next page about the following.

God has called you to serve Him and be on mission for Him, but He is not calling you to serve Him in order to earn your way into His favor. Adam and Eve rested on the first day of their lives, and Israel ate the Passover (a high Sabbath) before they attacked Jericho. You are called to be in covenant relationship with God, to enjoy Him, before you are called to work. This is what consecration means. Reflect on your life and see if there are any areas where you are relying on what you do to please God. Pray to God and ask for forgiveness if you are working to find peace rather than offering yourself to God and being His child first and working from that basis.

Unit 6: The Conquest

Lesson 6.2

EVALUATION

1. What is conquest all about in the Bible? _____
_____
_____

2. What does conquest mean for us? _____
_____
_____

3. What did God have Israel do to be prepared for conquest? _____
_____
_____
_____

4. What does consecrate mean?_____
_____
_____

5. What did God have Israel do to bring down the walls of Jericho? _____
_____
_____
_____

6. Why did God not have the Israelites just attack Jericho and help them tear down the walls? _____
_____
_____

LESSON 6.3

Moral Failure Impeded Conquest: Ai Routed Israel, but God Redeemed

UNIT 6

THE STORY

Lesson Theme - Achan retained possessions devoted to God, bringing defeat upon Israel.

In the conquest, Israel engaged in a special type of war called *herem* warfare. This kind of war was only to be waged against the Canaanites and Amalekites living in the promised land. The word *herem* means "devoted things." The devoted things were consecrated to God and either treated as an ascension offering (completely burned with holy fire from the tabernacle) or were given to the tabernacle (this was the case with gold, silver and other plunder). In this way, *herem* warfare, or holy war, was an extension of worship: God dictated what was to be offered to Him as *herem* (it varied from battle to battle), and to fail to follow God's instructions was to steal God's meat off His altar (much like what Ananias and Sapphira were guilty of much later).

In this lesson, we find out that Achan kept some of the devoted things at Jericho back for himself, and his sin led to Ai's defeat of Israel and the loss of 36 men. The moral failure of one man brought serious consequences for the entire nation. Because of Achan's sin, he and his entire family died, but the nation was restored and went back to defeat Ai. The main point of this lesson is that you have to deal with your own sin (crush the serpent inside) before you can defeat the enemy (crush the enemy-serpent).

Israel approached the initial battle with Ai (Josh 7:2-5) without following God's instructions. God had given Israel very specific directions about how to defeat Jericho, and Israel had followed them carefully; but when they went to battle against Ai, they didn't even ask the Lord how they ought to go about it. They had become overconfident in their own strength. (Remember, in this conquest, *God* was giving them the land; they were not just taking it themselves.) So, in their arrogance, Israel attacked Ai with a small force of men and were defeated and routed.

OVERVIEW

Having defeated Jericho in a decisive battle, Israel started to become arrogant. They went after the next city, Ai, without seeking the Lord and sent only a few thousand men against the city, thinking it would be no problem to defeat them. Ai routed Israel, and 36 men died. Joshua cried out to the Lord, not knowing that there was hidden sin in Israel's camp: someone had stolen God's plunder from Jericho. God led Joshua to Achan, and his whole family was stoned and burned—the sin was dealt with. God led the Israelites back into battle against Ai, and this time, they won a decisive battle, crushing the head of Ai. Following this victory, they returned to Mt. Ebal to renew their covenant with the Lord.

SOURCE MATERIAL

- Joshua 7-8
- Proverbs 15:29
- Psalm 66

Unit 6: The Conquest

OBJECTIVES

Feel...

- a bit jarred at God's anger and reaction to Achan's sin.
- sadness that Israel so quickly turned from trusting God and relied upon themselves.
- excitement when Israel went to battle against Ai the second time and defeated them.

Understand...

- why it was such a significant sin for Achan to take devoted things.
- that Israel failed to seek God when they attacked Ai the first time.
- the importance of Israel maintaining an abiding relationship with the Lord.
- the nature of the consequences for Israel of Achan's sin.
- how Israel was able to defeat Ai the second time.
- the significance of what Israel did to the king of Ai.

Apply this understanding by...

- looking at your own life to see if you have an ongoing relationship with the Lord.
- evaluating your life to determine if you have a pattern of rigorous repentance.

Joshua was shocked and cried out to the Lord, but his prayer sounds more like something the first generation would have said in the wilderness when they longed to return to Egypt where life was easier. Joshua said, "Alas, LORD God, why have You brought this people over the Jordan at all—to deliver us into the hand of the Amorites to destroy us? Oh, that we had been content, and dwelt on the other side of the Jordan!" (Josh 7:7). God responded by telling Joshua to snap out of it, act like a leader, and deal with the sin of the people (Josh 7:10-15).

By this point, there had been plenty of time for Achan to come to grips with and confess what he had done in stealing God's devoted plunder, but he didn't. So Joshua brought the tribes forward, and Judah was selected. Each clan and family of Judah came forward until Achan was chosen. Finally, Achan admitted to what he had done, but it was too late. The people quarantined Achan's whole family since they had become infected with the sin; then, the people stoned, burned, and piled rocks over Achan, his family, and the devoted things Achan had taken, making them an offering to the Lord (Josh 7:24-25). The pile of rocks became a monument or a reminder of the sin of Achan and its consequences (Josh 7:26).

After Israel had dealt with Achan's sin, God gave them instructions on how to attack Ai. They were to bring the *whole* army of Israel and set an ambush behind the city. So Israel followed the Lord's instructions and set an ambush party on the west side of the city with the main camp on the east. Ai was confident after their last skirmish with Israel, so all the men came out against the main camp on the east and chased Israel who feigned to flee. Meanwhile, the ambush party on the west attacked the city and then attacked Ai's fighting force from behind, trapping them between the ambush party and the main force. The main force then turned back and attacked the army of Ai from the east. In this way, they secured a decisive victory over Ai (Josh 8:1-22).

Notice what the Israelites did with the king of Ai and how it relates to the big Story. Remember, the story of conquest is about crushing the seed of the serpent who has taken the land. The king of Ai was the city's *head;* symbolically, when the king of Ai was killed, the head of this serpent city was crushed. Joshua hung the king on a tree, showing that he was cursed by God. At sunset, they took his body and threw it down at the city gate and buried it under a pile of rocks (Josh 8:29). This would become a symbolic way of showing that the head of the enemy had been crushed: he would be hung on a tree, then taken down and buried. The pile of rocks became a monument of the defeat of the enemy, just like the pile of rocks over Achan's body had become a monument reminding the people that their own sin had been dealt with.

Dealing with the shock
This lesson is a bit jarring. Up until now in the book of Joshua, the people had been faithful and obedient, and God had blessed them. We are not expecting such a big setback so soon. They were routed by the second city they attacked.

Furthermore, when we find out what it was that ignited God's anger, it doesn't sound like that big of a deal. And why would God punish the whole nation for one man's sin, not to mention: kill his whole family?

Don't try to justify God's behavior to yourself by saying, "God is not *really* like that; He doesn't punish a whole community for the sins of one man; and He doesn't kill whole families for the sins of their fathers... this story is an exception." Well, sometimes God does punish corporately the sins of one man, and sometimes He does extend the consequences from the father to his whole family: *that is part of the point of this lesson.*

Remember, in this curriculum, you will go through the *whole* Story. The story of Achan is one story in the grand narrative that tells about a merciful God who came to save the world. You are going to get a balanced picture of God as you go through the whole Bible. But for now, let this story stand on it's own; it is a lot to take, but there is an important truth here: our God is a consuming fire (Heb 12:29).

APPLICATION

Israel was harboring secret sin which led to their defeat at Ai; when they sought the Lord and dealt with their sin, He led them into a decisive battle against their enemy. We are called to the mission of spreading the gospel to the whole world, but if we try to execute our mission while harboring sin, we open ourselves up to an attack from the enemy and will experience significant setback.

There are two lines of application from this lesson. The first one is to learn from Joshua and Israel's failures; they should have sought the Lord *before* they went into battle and dealt with the sin when the consequences would have been lesser. This type of behavior requires an ongoing and abiding relationship with the Lord: we have to make space in our lives for a relationship with God *before* battle. The second line of application is to learn from what Israel did right: they dealt fully and decisively with sin in their midst once God revealed it. When God reveals to us that we have been harboring sin we *must* deal with it fully: cut out the cancer or it will spread. When we are confronted with our own sin, the temptation will be to confess it, but secretly hold onto it; God wants it gone.

Unit 6: The Conquest

ACTIVITIES

1. Map It. In the space below, or on a separate paper if you need more space, create a map/drawing from scratch, depicting the battle against Ai. Show on the map where the ambush party was hiding (on the west), where the main camp was (on the north), where they trapped the men of Ai and defeated them, and where they buried the king of Ai under stones. Be creative in your drawing: draw a walled city for Ai, not just a dot on a map; draw tents and stick figures for the camp of Israel, etc.

2. Journal Time: Crushing the Serpent Inside. You must crush the serpent inside the camp before you can crush the head of the enemy. God has called you to mission, but you have to do your own heart work first. The key to this is to have an ongoing, abiding relationship with the Lord. There are no shortcuts here, you have to actually talk to Him and hear from Him everyday.

Do you have a habit of regular prayer and seeking the Lord? If not, think about what you might do to set up something consistent in your life. Write a sentence explaining what something consistent would look like in your life. Start simple; maybe just praying the Lord's prayer everyday. _____

_____

_____

When you do fail, God wants to deal quickly and thoroughly with your sin. Think about a time in the recent past when God showed a sin in your life. How did you do in repenting of it? Did it come back to bite you after you had already repented? What should you do differently the next time to make sure the sin is dealt with? _____

_____

_____

_____

Lesson 6.3

EVALUATION

1. Explain Achan's sin and why it was such a big deal. _____

2. What did Israel do wrong before they attacked Ai the first time? _____

3. What could Israel have done to prevent losing 36 men at Ai? _____

4. What happened to Achan on account of his sin? _____

5. How did Israel defeat Ai the second time? _____

6. What did Israel do to the king of Ai? _____

7. What is the significance of what they did to the king? _____

LESSON 6.4

The Gibeonite Deception and Israel's Defeat of the Southern Amorite Alliance

UNIT 6

THE STORY

Lesson Theme - God was merciful to Israel even when they faltered.

This lesson is about God's mercy. God gave Israel victory, even though, by making peace with Gibeon, they disobeyed His command to destroy all the Amorites. Israel stumbled; they should have sought the Lord when the Gibeonites approached them to make peace. But after they fell, they got up, dusted themselves off, and were faithful to the treaty they had made even though it was made under false pretenses. In spite of Israel's error, God honored their faithfulness and used their new covenant with the Gibeonites to bring about the defeat of the Amorite alliance and ultimately, the entirety of southern Canaan.

This lesson starts with a warning of an impending all-out war against a united army of Canaanites (Josh 9:1-2). It is easy to skip over these two verses, but they are really important. Joshua 9:1 describes an alliance that encompassed the entire land of Canaan. The Canaanites were preparing a massive army to wipe Israel out. Israel's peace treaty with the Gibeonites plays a significant role in this story because it caused this united army to break up and led to Israel's victory in the south. Had this alliance successfully come together, they would have been a united army perhaps 10 to 20 times the size of Israel's and would have presented an incredible challenge to Israel's conquest of the land. It would be much easier for Israel to defeat the Canaanites one city at a time on a campaign through the land than to take them on all at once. In the next lesson, we will see Israel face a large united northern

OVERVIEW

Israel had defeated Ai and Jericho, inciting all the peoples in the land of Canaan to unite against them in battle. The Gibeonites, however, had a different plan. They deceived Israel into thinking they were from a far country. Israel made a peace treaty with Gibeon without consulting the Lord. When Israel found out they had been deceived, they confronted the Gibeonites, but still remained faithful to their oath. In response to this peace treaty, five Amorite kings from the south attacked Gibeon *not expecting Israel to help them*. This attack began the process of breaking up the nationwide alliance. Gibeon called on Israel to help, and so Israel marched all night and routed the enemy in the day. God caused the sun to stand still while Israel tracked down all the men to kill them. Meanwhile, the five kings were found hiding in a cave. Joshua had stones placed over the entrance to the cave while the battle went on. Later, they took the kings out of the cave, stepped on their necks and hung them on trees to die. At sunset, they took their bodies down, put them back in the cave, and covered it with stones as a memorial. They then struck down the city of Makkedah and began a campaign through the now weakened southern part of Canaan.

SOURCE MATERIAL

- Joshua 9:1-10:28
- Psalm 9
- Proverbs 24:16

Unit 6: The Conquest

OBJECTIVES

Feel...

- exasperation that Israel again didn't seek the Lord's counsel.
- relief that Israel kept their oath to the Gibeonites even though they had been deceived.
- joy that Israel was so victorious over the kings of the south.

Understand...

- why it was wrong for Israel to make peace with Gibeon.
- how the peace treaty with Gibeon led to victory in southern Canaan.
- the time sequence and geographic locations of the movements of Israel, Gibeon and the Amorite alliance.
- the symbolic significance of what Joshua did to the five kings who hid in the cave.

Apply this understanding by...

- considering areas in your own life where you have failed in your walk with the Lord, but God worked it out for good anyway.
- thanking God for His mercy in those areas.
- determining what faithfulness looks like in your own life.

alliance, but this alliance was perhaps half the size it might have been on account of how the Gibeonite treaty broke apart the southern force.

Gibeon, however, didn't join in the alliance of Canaanites. Instead, they decided to try to trick Israel into making peace with them (Josh 9:3-5). Israel again failed to seek the Lord, and as a result, they believed the lie and made a treaty of peace with the Gibeonites (Josh 9:14-15). (And, remember, the Gibeonites were among the peoples God had commanded Israel to completely destroy [Deut 20:17]). When Israel discovered that they had been deceived, they were tempted to attack Gibeon; instead, Israel remained faithful to their covenant and kept peace with them (Josh 9:16-18). Instead of destroying the Gibeonites, Israel made them servants (woodcutters and water-carriers—Josh 9:20-21), which was a step further than simply being at peace with them and put the Gibeonites under the protection of Israel (slave owners were responsible for their slaves' well-being).

Of course, the Amorites (who were among the Canaanite nations united against Israel) did not appreciate their brothers in Gibeon (who were also Amorites) making peace with Israel. So, instead of coming together with all the other nations to attack Israel, Adoni-Zedek, the king of Jerusalem (himself an Amorite) gathered a smaller alliance of Amorite kings and attacked Gibeon (Josh 10:1-5). He was certainly not expecting Israel to come to the aid of Gibeon, but as servants of Israel, the Gibeonites were entitled to Israel's protection. So the Gibeonites called on Israel to help them in their battle against the five Amorite kings of the south. Israel heard their cry; this time, Israel consulted the Lord, and He told them that they would have victory. They routed the enemy, and God caused a hailstorm to strike the Amorites down as they were fleeing, killing even more than Israel struck with the sword (Josh 10:6-11). But that's not all. Israel needed more time to route and kill their enemies, so Joshua asked the Lord to cause the sun to stand still in the sky, and it did—for a full day (Josh 10:12-13). Truly God was on Israel's side!

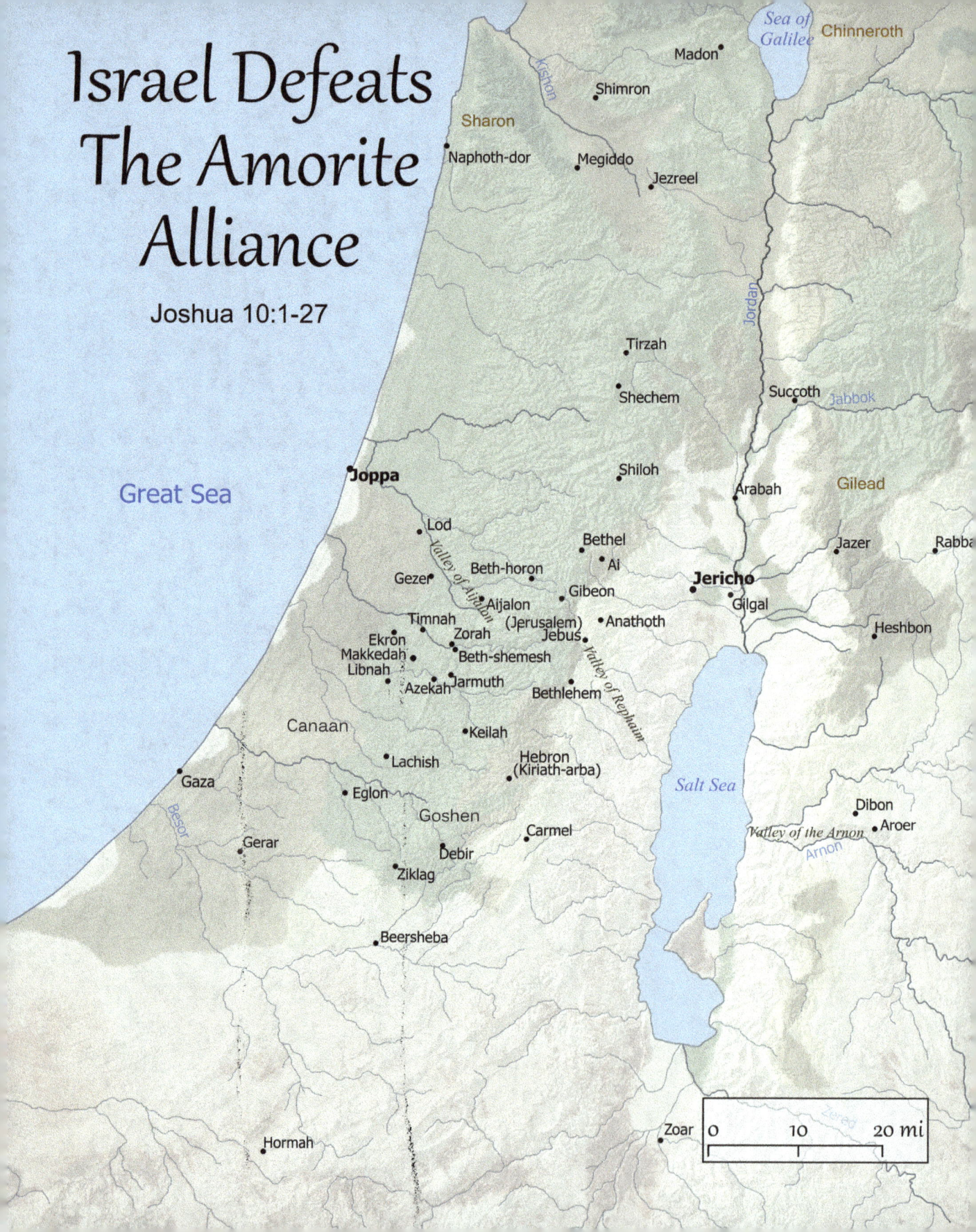

When the Israelite army returned to their camp at Gilgal, Joshua was told that the five Amorite kings were found hiding in the cave at Makkedah. Joshua saw his chance to destroy the armies of these cities. Their fighting men were running and afraid, and their leadership had abandoned them. So Joshua's men trapped the kings in the cave and chased down their armies to kill every man (Josh 10:16-20).

When the Israelites had finished the battle, they returned to the cave of the five kings. Joshua instructed them to take the kings out of the cave and had the captains of Israel stand on their necks, symbolically crushing their heads (Josh 10:22-24). Joshua used this picture to teach his men courage: "...thus the LORD will do to all your enemies against whom you fight" (Josh 10:25). Joshua then killed the kings and hung their bodies on trees, symbolically cursing them. He took them down at sunset and buried them in the cave, covering it with stones, which became a memorial of the defeat of the kings of the south (Josh 10:27). These kings are the serpents of this story whose heads were crushed by the seed-people.

The rest of Joshua 10 chronicles the southern sweep. Having built the confidence of his men, Joshua and the Israelite army continued in conquest in the south, going from city to city, destroying their enemies wherever they went.

The relationship between the Canaanites
There are a number of people Israel encountered in their conquest of the land; they were all Canaanites (descendants of Canaan, Noah's grandson), and over time they spread out into the land. The Amorites, for example, were grouped in the southern hill country of Canaan. So you might think of the Amorite cities as brothers to each other and cousins of the Hittites, another group of Canaanites. Genesis 10:15-18 says that Canaan was the father of Sidon, the Hittites, the Jebusites, the Amorites, the Girgashites, the Hivites, Arkites, and Sinites as well as the Arvadites, Zemarites and Hamathites. While the Gibeonites are not mentioned in the Genesis 10 list, they were also Canaanites.

The one major exception, and this will be important later, were the Philistines. They were *not* Canaanites. They were descendants of Mizraim and were therefore Egyptians by ancestry (Gen 10:13).

APPLICATION

Israel should have sought the Lord when the Gibeonites approached them to make peace, but they didn't. However, unlike their failure to seek the Lord before attacking Ai, they didn't experience a setback in their conquest. Rather, their treaty with the Gibeonites provided occasion for them to break the Canaanite alliance in two and defeat the kings of the south. When Israel realized that they had been deceived, they didn't back out of their covenant of peace with the Gibeonites, even though they wanted to. Rather, they accepted where they were and honored God in it. As a result, God used this situation for His glory even though it was caused by Israel's negligence.

God is perfect, but He is not a hard perfectionist. When we sin, God isn't looking to find some way to trap us in our sin; He wants us to confess and act in righteousness, even if it hurts. He can use even our failures to work out our deliverance. If we view God as a hard and punishing father, we will self-destruct, adding sin upon sin. God will meet us and deliver us wherever we are as we follow Him.

Unit 6: The Conquest

ACTIVITIES

1. Draw It. When Israel defeated the armies of the five kings of the south, they went through a sort of symbolic ritual to crush the heads of their kings.

1. They temporarily imprisoned them in their grave.
2. They defeated their armies.
3. They pulled them out and stepped on their necks, symbolically crushing their heads.
4. They killed them.
5. They hung them on trees (a symbolic crucifixion).
6. They buried them in the cave, piling stones up over the mouth to mark their death as a permanent solution.

Draw each of the six steps of the head-crushing in the space below or on a separate piece of paper if you need more space. This should entail six sequential drawings.

2. Map It. Represent the movements of the Amorite alliance, the Gibeonites and Israel's army on the map on page 32, using arrows and indicating what the arrows mean with text. See Joshua 10:1-28.

3. Journal Time. God uses not only the good things we do to bring about victory in our lives, but sometimes He redeems mistakes we make for our own victory, as long as we "go and sin no more" (John 8:11) like Israel did with Gibeon. Write about the following.

Lesson 6.4

- Think of a time where God has used a mistake you made to bring about good things in your life. Thank God for that.
- Is there an area of your life where you have stumbled recently? What do you need to do to be faithful in response to your failure?
- Spend some time praying that God would use your mistakes to work out His plan for victory in your life.

EVALUATION

1. Why was it wrong for Israel to make peace with Gibeon? _____

2. How did the peace treaty help Israel defeat southern Canaan? _____

3. What did Joshua do to the five kings who hid at the cave at Makkedah? _____

4. What is the symbolic significance of these things? _____

LESSON 6.5

Israel Conquered and Divided the Land

UNIT 6

THE STORY

Lesson Theme: Israel entered into the rest.
This lesson provides a final contrast between the first generation, who did not enter the rest (Ps 95) and the second generation who (1) trusted in the Lord, (2) conquered the land, (3) received their inheritance, and (4) entered into the rest. The takeaway from this lesson is that victory and rest *are* possible, even promised by God, to those who trust in Him. God did not just give us negative examples in the Bible; we have here an example of conquest, victory and rest. This is a message of hope for Christians today. We *can... must* enter the rest.

The first 10 chapters of the book of Joshua present in much detail the conquest of Jericho, Ai, the Gibeonite deception, and the battle with the Amorite alliance. The remainder of the conquest and the defeat of numerous cities is chronicled in much less detail in the second half of chapter 10 and the first part of chapter 11. Having defeated the five Amorite kings in the south, the southern conquest came quickly and easily. The alliance had been broken, and the Israelites faced little united resistance in the southern campaign.

As we learned in the last lesson, Israel never had to face a nationwide alliance of Canaanites. The treaty with the Gibeonites caused the Amorites to split off of the greater alliance to attack Gibeon. Israel was able to defeat them, leading to the southern campaign. The northern Canaanites, however, were still able to pull together a substantial united force. Hazor was the largest and most fortified city in the northern part of Ca-

OVERVIEW

Israel gained control of the southern portion of Canaan, provoking the northern Canaanites to unite in battle against Israel. Jabin, king of Hazor, gathered a huge army. Israel didn't wait for them to attack, however. God said Israel would have the victory, so the Israelite army marched on the camp of the Canaanites at the waters of Merom and defeated them, chasing them down and destroying their cities. Thus, Israel gained control of the northern part of the land. They then swept through central and southern Canaan, killing the Anakites (the giants). All that was left were the Philistines in the southwest and pockets of Canaanites throughout the land. Joshua allotted land to the tribes of Israel, and they went in and took possession of the land, entering into rest.

SOURCE MATERIAL

- Joshua 10:28-22:34
- Psalm 9
- Proverbs 2:7

naan. Jabin, the king of Hazor, was able to unite a great number of cities to bring battle against Israel (Josh 11:1-5)—"as numerous as the sand on the seashore" (Josh 11:4, NIV). They gathered at the waters of Merom in the north to march against Israel. But they never had to march; God told Joshua to take them on in battle because He would give Israel victory. So Israel brought a surprise attack against them at the waters of

Unit 6: The Conquest

OBJECTIVES

Feel...

- joy that Israel was victorious over the Canaanites.
- hopeful that you too can experience victory in your own life.

Understand...

- the sequence and geography of the southern and northern campaigns as well as the final sweep through the land to defeat the Anakites.
- what it meant for Israel to have peace and enter into rest.
- the locations of the land allotments for the tribes of Israel.

Apply this understanding by...

- thanking God for the hope of victory in your life.
- entrusting your future to God.

Merom, chased them down, killed them all and took all of their cities (Josh 11:6-15). This left Israel in control of northern Canaan.

Following this victory, the army of Israel made their way south again, destroying the Anakites (Josh 11:21-22). These were the giants who had instilled fear in ten of the twelve spies of the first generation. Defeating these enemies surely brought Joshua (and Caleb) great joy. The Anakites were not Canaanites but were perhaps related to the Philistines. In any case, the Anakites who remained went and dwelt in the cities of the Philistines, which were not taken by Israel during the conquest.

Israel was now left with substantial control of the land. They took *all* the land (Josh 11:23). There were, of course, pockets of Canaanites still living and the Philistines in the southwest part of the land, but it was expected that when each tribe went to claim their inheritance, they would defeat any enemies that were left there. Chapter 11 ends with the words, "Then the land rested from war" (Josh 11:23). God had given victory to the second generation, and they entered into the rest.

What remained now was for the land to be allotted to each of the tribes and for them to settle in their lands and enjoy what God had given to them. So Joshua allotted a share of land to each tribe. The Levites, of course, did not receive any land. As priests, they were given cities in the land of each of the tribes. The allotments are given in great detail in Joshua 13-21, but the important thing is to understand the big picture of the land divisions. See the map for how the land was divided among the tribes.

APPLICATION

Hope is what you want to take out of this lesson. This lesson deals with major Bible concepts such as peace, rest and inheritance. This lesson gives us pictures of where we are headed. The first piece of good news here is that victory is possible. Many Christians believe that they will always struggle in the same ways. Many believe that anxiety and fear are just a part of life; living in peace is a pipe-dream. No. Israel did actually enter into the rest, and we too can enter into the rest as we trust in the Lord. God gives victory to those who are upright (Prov 2:7).

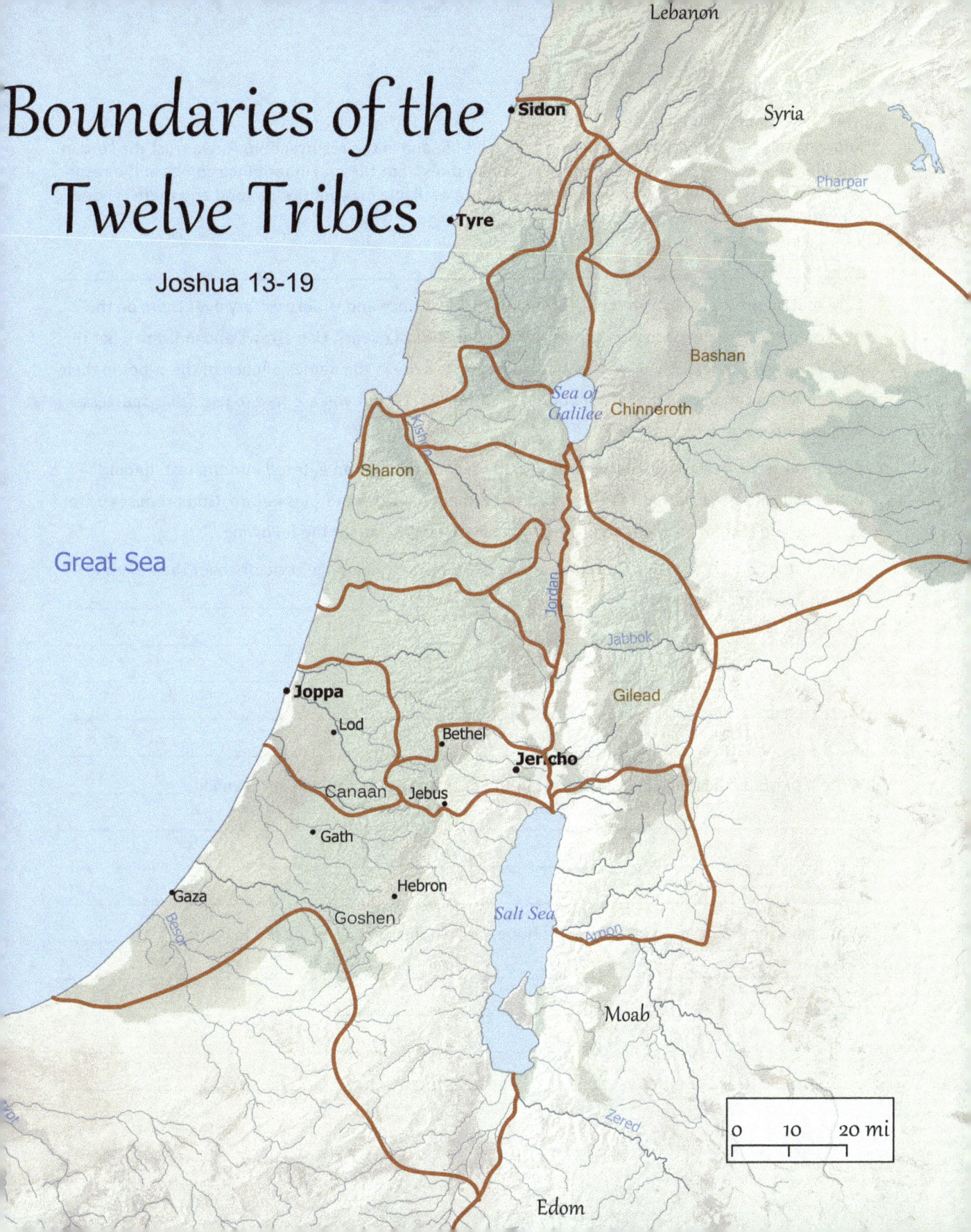

Unit 6: The Conquest

Knowing this rest is possible provides hope for this life and in the resurrection. As we trust the Lord in this life, we will receive an experience of victory and rest, but the real inheritance comes in the resurrection when we receive our reward. There is peace available for you; God is good and there is hope for your future no matter your past.

ACTIVITIES

1. Map It. Represent the movements of the northern alliance and Israel's victory over them on the map on page 38. Refer to Joshua 11 to find the sequence of events. Use arrows and indicate what the arrows mean with text. Then, on the map on page 41, write in the names of each of the tribes in their appropriate locations. All the information is in Joshua 13-19, but you are free to use other sources as well (online maps, Bible atlas, etc.)

2. Journal Time. God gave Israel victory, and the second generation entered into the rest, finding peace and a home in the land God had promised them many generations before. God promises victory, peace and rest for each Christian who trusts in Him. Write about the following.

Write a short prayer thanking God for what He did for Israel, giving them victory over their enemies and an inheritance in the land.

Write a prayer confessing any lack of trust in the possibility of victory in your own life.

Write a prayer thanking God that there is hope, both in this life and in the life to come.

Lesson 6.5

EVALUATION

1. Summarize Israel's southern campaign. _____
_____
_____

2. Summarize Israel's victory in the north. _____
_____
_____
_____

3. What does it mean that Israel had peace and entered into rest? _____
_____
_____

4. Who were the Anakites? _____
_____
_____

5. Was Israel able to defeat the Anakites? _____

UNIT 7: THE JUDGES

Instead of defeating the remaining Canaanites who lived in the land, the generations following the conquest chose to coexist with them, so God ceased to fight for Israel. Instead, He made making their Canaanite neighbors a source of strife. Israel entered into a cycle: they would get seduced into worshiping their neighbors' idols, God would give them to their neighbors to be oppressed, they would cry out to God to save them, God would send a judge to deliver them, the judge would crush the heads of their enemies and all would be well...until Israel fell into idolatry again.

Mostly, the judges were godly men, but God remembered His promise to use the seed of the woman to crush the serpent's head, and so during this time He also raised up a succession of head-crushing women. Deborah, a female judge, prophet and military leader, set the stage for another woman, Jael, to crush the head of the serpent by driving a tent-peg through his head. In a subsequent story, an unnamed woman crushed the head of another serpent, Abimelech, when she dropped an upper millstone on his head.

To close this sorry period in Israel's history, God sent two barren women sons at about the same time. The sons, Samuel and Samson, operated in different spheres: Samuel in the sanctuary and Samson on the battlefield. Samson married a Philistine woman, which resulted in a chance to kill a lot of Philistines, including 1,000 men whose heads he crushed with the jawbone of a donkey. Samson continued to lust after Philistine women and eventually ended up with Delilah, who convinced him to tell her the secret of his strength. She cut his hair, and the Philistines captured him, gouging out his eyes and imprisoning him. He remained in prison until the Philistines threw a big party at the temple of Dagon and brought out their vanquished enemy Samson to entertain the party guests. By this time, Samson's hair had regrown, and God gave him his strength back. Samson pulled down the temple on his own head, in the process killing 3,000 Philistines, including their five kings, effectively beheading the nation and preparing the way for Israel's deliverance from Philistine domination.

The Judges Cycle: Slavery and Deliverance

Enemy	Years of Slavery	Judge	Years of Deliverance and Rest	Scripture (Judges)
Moab	18	Ehud	80	3:12-31
Canaan	20	Deborah	40	4:1-5:31
Midian	7	Gideon	40	6:1-8:28
Ammon	18	Jephthah	6	10:6-12:7
Philistia	40	Samson	20	13:1-16:31

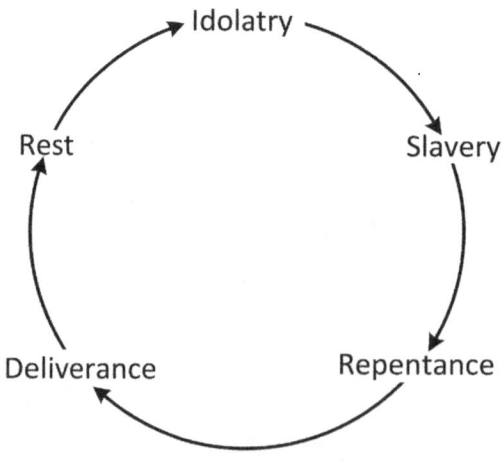

LESSON 7.1

Israel Failed to Take the Land and Fell into a Cycle of Slavery and Deliverance

UNIT 7

THE STORY

Lesson theme - The Judges cycle

In the conquest, Israel had defeated many of the major cities and kings who lived in Canaan, but many more cities remained to be defeated. At the end of the book of Joshua, the tribes were sent to take possession of their allotted territories, which meant ongoing battles for the armies of each of the tribes. Some tribes fared better than others, but the overall pattern was that Israel held some territory, but allowed their enemies to remain in possession of a good bit of it; they were complacent in finishing the job. Israel was, therefore, in a place of ongoing unrest. Following the conquest, Israel's enemies were defeated, scattered and disoriented, and Israel was at peace; but as Israel was dividing up the land and taking possession of their territories, their enemies regrouped and presented a new challenge to Israel.

God observed Israel's pattern of complacency and spoke to them at Bokim (Judg 2:1-4). God had delivered them from Egypt, brought them safely into the land, and gave them their inheritance; and they got lazy. God told them that He would no longer go before them and drive out their enemies; rather, their enemies would stay in the land and be "thorns in [Israel's] side" (Judg 2:3).

During this period, Israel was not united under a central government. Rather, they were united under a central place of worship: they set up the tabernacle at Shiloh for their united worship of Yahweh (Josh 18:1). When a military ruler was needed, God would send a judge. Judges were

OVERVIEW

After defeating many of their enemies and taking control of the land, the tribes of Israel split up to take possession of their respective territories. Each tribe was to defeat the remaining Canaanites who lived in their land; instead, the Israelites defeated some of the Canaanites and decided to live among the rest. The Lord was displeased and rebuked the Israelites for not defeating their enemies. He told them He would no longer drive their enemies out before them, but would make them a source of strife. So Israel settled into a vicious cycle in the land: they would fall into idolatry and worship the false gods of their neighbors; God would make them slaves of their enemies; Israel would cry out for God to save them; God would send a judge to deliver them; Israel would fall into idolatry again. And so the cycle continued. The judges were godly head-crushers sent by God to deliver Israel. The story of the first major judge, Ehud, illustrates Israel's cycle perfectly, and ends with Ehud crushing Eglon, the head of Moab, by driving a sword into his body.

SOURCE MATERIAL

- Judges 1-3
- Psalm 7
- Proverbs 14:30

temporary rulers whose authority was normally confined to a geographical region. Judges were head-crushers. When Israel cried out to be de-

Unit 7: The Judges

OBJECTIVES

Feel...

- sad that the tribes of Israel failed to take full possession of the land and fell into complacency.
- exasperated by Israel's vicious cycle during the period of the Judges.
- joy that there were faithful people (especially the head-crushing judges) during this period.

Understand...

- why God brought the judgment of the Judges cycle upon Israel.
- the sequence of repeated events in the Judges cycle.
- how complacency leads to idolatry, and idolatry leads to slavery.
- how eager God was to deliver Israel when they would cry out to Him.
- the story of Ehud and Eglon and how it illustrates the Judges cycle.

Apply this understanding by...

- identifying areas of idolatry in your life.
- seeing how that idol has made you a slave.
- repenting of idol-worship, so that you can be delivered from slavery.

livered from the Canaanites, God would send a judge to crush the head of their enemies.

The Judges cycle
The period of the Judges was one of great temptation for Israel; it was a time of testing and purification. The second generation had died off, and the third generation came of age. They had not been a part of the journeys in the wilderness nor a part of the conquest. In short, they did not know God. Instead of faithfully worshiping Yahweh, they worshiped the false gods of the Canaanites. We see a pattern repeated over and over in the book of Judges, a cycle that is spelled out specifically in Judges 2. Grasping this pattern is important to understanding the book of Judges.

1. Israel would worship the false gods of the Canaanites.
2. God would cause them to be defeated and become slaves of the Canaanites.
3. Israel would cry out to God and repent of their sin in worshiping the false gods.
4. God would send a judge who would crush the enemy's head and set Israel free.
5. Israel would not listen to their judges, and the cycle would repeat.

The main point in this lesson has two sides. On the negative side, complacency leads to idolatry, which in turn (in a reap-what-you-sow sort of way), leads to slavery. On the positive side, God was eager to raise a judge to crush the heads of Israel's enemies when they repented; *even though* they had developed a pattern of complacency/idolatry.

Judges overview
In addition to the cycle presented above, study the chart on page 46 to get and overview of the book of Judges. You should know who each of the judges were. We will not have time to cover them all, so a thirty-thousand foot picture of the book will be important. It is important to understand that the book of Judges is not sequential. Many of the judges overlapped and were working in different regions of Israel.

All told, there are fifteen judges who receive mention in the book of Judges, but many of them are just mentioned in passing. The five listed above are the major focus of the book of Judges.

Ehud and Eglon
The Judges cycle is illustrated well in the story of Ehud and Eglon (Judg 3:12-30). The story starts out by saying, "And the children of Israel again did evil in the sight of the LORD. So the LORD strengthened Eglon king of Moab against Israel, because they had done evil in the sight of the LORD" (Judg 3:12). This statement illustrates the first point of the cycle given above. So Eglon gathered an army including Moabites, Ammonites and Amalekites, attacked Israel and gained victory over them. Thus, the Israelites were made slaves of Eglon king of Moab (Judg 3:13)—the second point of the cycle. In time (18 years, to be exact), the Israelites cried out to the Lord, and He raised up a judge, a deliverer named Ehud (Judg 3:14-15)—the third point of the cycle.

Remember, we are talking about crushing heads here; the word "head" is often used with a double sense in the Old Testament. In Judges, the king or military ruler was seen as the "head" of Israel's enemies; the judges would attack that ruler. Sometimes, the "head's" actual head was crushed, but often he was killed in some other fashion. In the story of Ehud and Eglon, Ehud killed Eglon with a sword to the gut (Judg 3:21).

Read Judges 3:15-25 to get the story of how Ehud killed Eglon. A couple of explanatory notes: (1) tribute money was basically a slave labor tax. When one nation ruled over another, they used their authority to heavily tax them. When Ehud brought the tribute money to Eglon (Judg 3:17), he was paying Israel's slave taxes. (2) Notice that Ehud was left handed (Judg 3:15); this feature meant that he could hide a short sword on his right side, and it would not be noticed since those inspecting him would look for a longer sword on his left side.

After Ehud "crushed" the head of the Moabites, the people of Israel responded to Ehud's call and went to finish off the enemy. They struck down about 10,000 Moabites and made them subject to Israel. After this victory, Israel experienced 80 years of peace (Judg 3:28-30).

APPLICATION

There is a very important point of application about idolatry in this lesson. Judges 2:12-14 says that Israel forsook God and went after the gods of their neighbors, and so God gave them over as slaves to the peoples whose gods they went after. Romans 6:16 tells us, "Do you not know that to whom you present yourselves slaves to obey, you are that one's slaves whom you obey…?" And this is exactly what happened to Israel; they became slaves of the gods they worshiped.

It works the same for us. Even good things can become idols when we worship them above God. Proverbs 14:30 (NIV) says, "A heart at peace gives life to the body, but envy rots the bones." When we desire something more than God, it leads to envy; envy makes us slaves and leads to misery.

Unit 7: The Judges

ACTIVITIES

1. Draw It: The Judges Cycle. In the space below, illustrate the Judges cycle visually—draw each stage of the cycle in a circle leading back to the beginning. Use keywords in your diagram: (1) Idolatry, (2) Slavery, (3) Repentance, (4) Deliverance (head-crushing), (5) Rest. You can also add a simple illustration for each keyword in the circle with a little icon drawing (for instance: a man bowing to his knees to pray at the repentance part, or a head being crushed on the deliverance part).

2. Journal Time. Reflect on God's mercy to Israel in being eager to deliver Israel when they cried out to Him. Write a short prayer thanking the Lord for His goodness to Israel, and to all of us as well.

Pray and ask God to reveal any areas where you are idolizing something; this could even be something good. We often idolize people we love, a hobby or favorite past-time, or possessions. If the thought of not getting what you are hoping for brings feelings of panic you might be idolizing that thing. What did God reveal to you?

Lesson 7.1

If you have identified an idol in your life, write a short prayer of repentance in the space below asking God to deliver you from slavery to your idol. _____
_____
_____
_____
_____

EVALUATION

1. What did Israel do that caused God to stop fighting for them and bring a cycle of judgment and deliverance upon them? _____
_____
_____

2. What is the Judges cycle? _____
_____
_____

3. Was God faithful to deliver the Israelites when they repented?_____
_____
_____

4. How was Ehud able to kill Eglon? _____
_____
_____

5. How was Ehud's killing of Eglon a head-crushing? _____
_____
_____

6. How long did Israel have peace after Ehud's victory?_____
_____
_____

LESSON 7.2

The Head-Crushing Women of Judges

THE STORY

Lesson Theme - Head-crushing women

In the garden of Eden, it was Adam's responsibility to protect his wife, but he let her down. Instead of resisting and defeating the serpent, he stood by while his wife was deceived. On account of Adam's failure, God promised to the woman that she would bring life to the head-crusher. This promise (that a head-crusher would come from Eve) is played out in two separate but related themes in the Bible. First, we get story after story of women who gave birth to the head-crusher or promised son (Eve, Sarah, Hannah.... Mary). Second, we have stories of women who were head-crushers themselves, and these are the women we will learn about in this lesson. Ultimately, the bride of Christ, the Church, is the woman who will crush the the head of the serpent; in the New Testament, Paul, writing to the Church says, "The God of peace will crush Satan under your feet shortly" (Rom 16:20).

The main point in this lesson is that women are at the heart of what God is doing to defeat the enemy. God uses women as well as men to crush the head of the serpent. The women in this lesson: Deborah, Jael, and the unnamed woman who crushed Abimelech's head are called courageous and faithful warriors.

Deborah and Jael

This story starts out with a repeat of the Judges cycle that we learned about in the last lesson. Ehud had brought Israel deliverance and they had peace for 80 years (Judg 3:30), but as soon as Ehud died, Israel did evil in the Lord's sight

OVERVIEW

God promised in Genesis 3:15 that a seed of the woman would crush the head of the serpent. Throughout the Bible, this principle is taught over and over, and on a number of occasions, it was the woman who directly crushed the head of the serpent. Deborah, a female judge, prophet and military leader, set the stage for another woman, Jael, to crush the head of the serpent by driving a tent-peg through his head. In a subsequent story, an unnamed woman crushed the head of another serpent, Abimelech, when she dropped an upper millstone on his head.

SOURCE MATERIAL

- Judges 4-9
- Judges 5 (a psalm within Judges)
- Proverbs 31:30

(Judg 4:1). So God sold them into slavery to Jabin, king of the Canaanites (Judg 4:2).

Deborah was the judge whom the Lord raised up to deliver Israel from the power of the Canaanites (Judg 4:4). Deborah is the only female judge in the book of Judges and one of the strongest female leaders in the Bible. She was not only responsible for leading Israel (including the men), she was also a prophetess. It is clear from the Old Testament, that female leadership at the national level was not the pattern, but it is also clear that there is nothing wrong with it

Unit 7: The Judges

OBJECTIVES

Feel...

- gratitude in seeing that God uses women in His battle against the enemy.
- joy in the victory the woman head-crushers brought against their enemies.

Understand...

- the significance of women in God's plan, both in giving life to head-crushers and in being head-crushers themselves.
- that Deborah was called by God to be a judge and prophet.
- that Barak, though he was the military leader, is a weaker character in the story than Deborah or Jael.
- that Jael was the hero and head-crusher in the story, not a murderer.
- how evil Abimelech was and what evil things he did.
- that an unnamed woman crushed his head (literally) with a stone.

Apply this understanding by...

- thanking God for women who are bold and fear the Lord.
- valuing the place women have in the Story (guys).
- being willing to pursue God's calling for you in your part of the Story (girls).

(this is contrasted with the Levitical priesthood which admitted *no* women, *ever*). God had called Deborah to this task because *she* was the one He wanted. God may put women in a position of authority over them, and they are not to despise what God has chosen to do.

Deborah had received a word from the Lord: Barak, from the tribe of Naphtali, was to organize a force to attack the Canaanites (Judg 4:6). The Canaanite army was led by a commander named Sisera, who was under Jabin, a king of Canaan. Barak was to assemble a force and attack Sisera and his army at the Kishon River. When Deborah told him this, he balked. He said, "I'll do it if you'll go with me" (Judg 4:8*), rather than, "If God says to, I am ready to serve Him." Because of Barak's response, Deborah told him that he would not enjoy the honor of crushing the head of the Canaanite army, Sisera. That glory would go to a woman instead (Judg 4:9).

So Barak went to battle and defeated the army of Sisera. Sisera, however, fled on foot. He went to the house of Heber the Kenite, who was a descendant of Moses' father-in-law, Jethro, which meant that Heber was a Midianite, not an Israelite. Heber had left the rest of his family who remained loyal to Israel and had made peace with Jabin and the Canaanites. The same was not true of his wife, Jael. Jael greeted Sisera and welcomed him into her home since Heber was away. She made Sisera comfortable, and he fell asleep... then she drove a tent-peg through his head and into the ground (Judg 4:17-22)!

It may be tempting to think that Jael murdered Sisera, but this is not the case. She was acting in a wartime situation with shrewd strategy, and she crushed the head of the serpent. Jael was the hero. Following this victory, Deborah wrote a song in celebration (Judg 5), and spoke of Jael as "most blessed among women" (Judg 5:24). Pay close attention to Judges 5:24-27 to see how the prophetess Deborah reflected on what Jael had done.

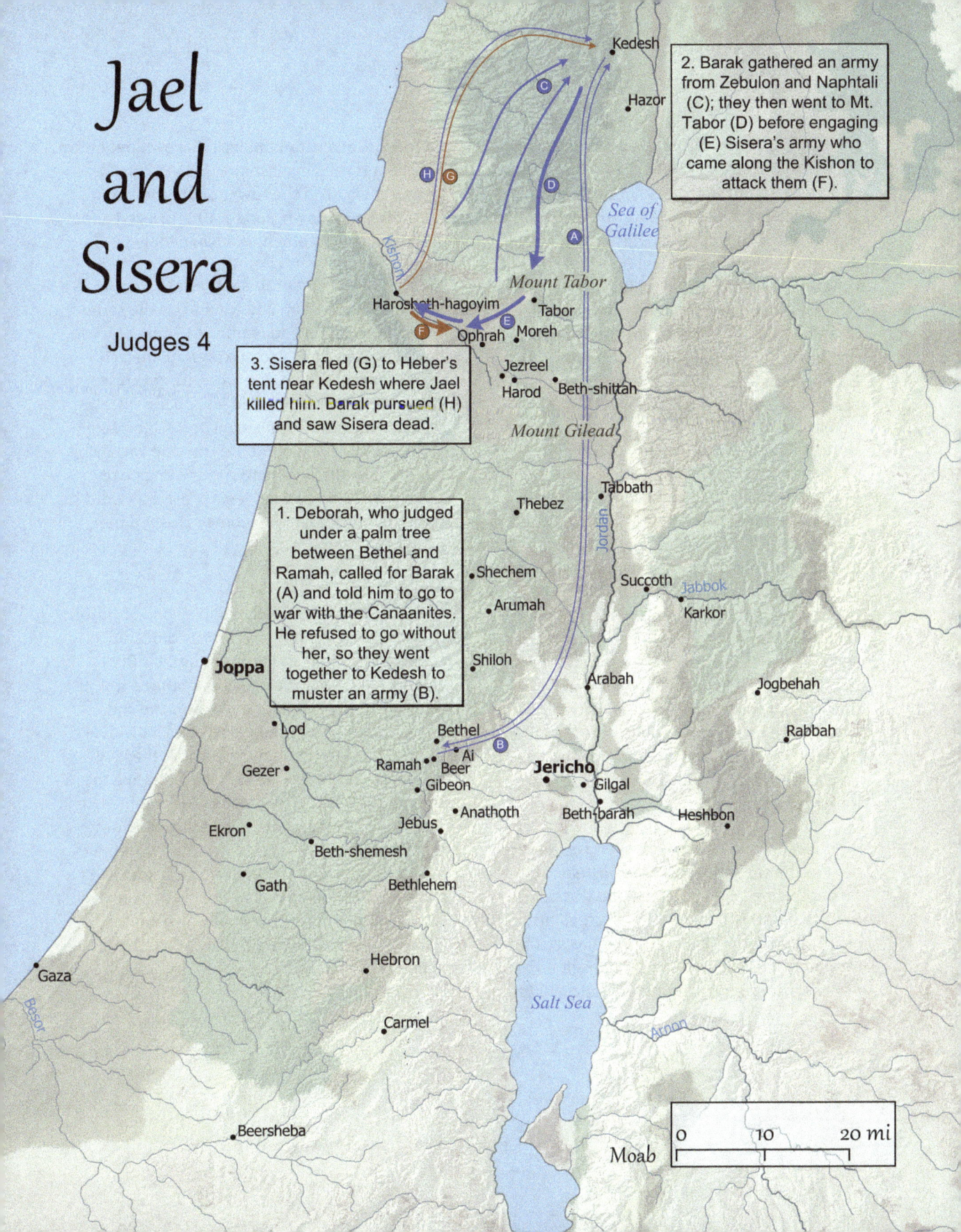

Unit 7: The Judges

Abimelech's head crushed by a woman
Following the story of Deborah and Jael, Israel had peace for 40 years. At that time, they again sinned against the Lord... and we have another repeat of the Judges cycle. This time the Midianites oppressed them, and when Israel cried out the Lord, He sent Gideon to deliver them. The story of Gideon and his defeat of the Midianites is really good, but for the purposes of this curriculum we are passing over it. The result is that God used Gideon to defeat the Midianites and bring peace to Israel.

Unfortunately, Gideon became proud and made a false idol out of gold and married lots and lots of women. In all, he had 70 sons. As soon as he died, Israel turned to all-out idol worship again (Judg 8:25-35). We don't know much about most of Gideon's sons, but Abimelech was a son born to Gideon by a prostitute in Shechem. There are two things of note about his name, "Abimelech." First, it was a Canaanite dynastic title (like Jabin). Second, its Hebrew meaning is "My father is the king." This tells us a couple of things. First, Gideon had gotten so infatuated with his own importance that he named his son "My father is the king." Second, with a name like Abimelech, he was destined to rule just like a cruel Canaanite king... and he did.

Abimelech was a *really* bad guy; he is the serpent in the story. But this time, instead of the serpent being a foreign power, he was an Israelite. The first thing he did was kill off all his brothers (Gideon's sons) and offer them as sacrifices (probably to Baal); then he set himself up as king of Israel (Judg 9:5-6). But before long, God started to work against Abimelech. His own people at Shechem turned against him. His response was to trap them all in the tower of Shechem and burn the thing down (Judg 9:49). He killed about 1,000 men and women; his own people!

Abimelech then went to another city that was revolting against him and tried to do the same thing. All the men and women of Thebez locked themselves in their strong tower. Abimelech tried to burn it down, but when he got close enough, a woman dropped an upper millstone on his head, cracking his skull open (Judg 10:52-53). It was a fatal wound. He knew he was dying, but didn't want anyone to say a woman had killed him, so he had his servant drive a sword through him. Again, the woman crushed the head of the serpent.

Additional notes
The Canaanites were led by Jabin, king of Hazor. In Lesson 6.5, we saw that Joshua defeated Hazor, killed Jabin and burned the city. This could sound like a contradiction, but really it just clues us in on what happened after the conquest. "Jabin" is not the name of an individual person, but is rather a dynastic title; the king of Hazor was always called "Jabin" just like the king of Egypt was always called "Pharaoh." After the defeat of Hazor, the many Canaanites who remained alive returned to the city and rebuilt it, setting up a king (Jabin) just like before. God allowed all of this to happen because Israel failed to take possession of the tribal inheritances (Judg 2:1-4). So now Israel had to face the same enemies all over again.

Lesson 7.2

APPLICATION

God created Adam to protect and provide for Eve, but so far in the story we have seen men, time and time again, mistreating women. Adam abdicated his responsibility to protect Eve; Abraham let Pharaoh and later Abimelech (an earlier one) have his wife; it goes on and on. On the other hand, God has consistently shown favor to women, even prostitutes (Tamar and Rahab). He made their acts of faithfulness key points in His Story of redemption as He brought about the Messiah. In this lesson, women are the heroes, playing the roles that are most often played by men (head-crushers and national leaders). In these stories, the roles of men and women are reversed, and it is glorious, not shameful in any way.

In our culture, women are often objectified, pornographied and lusted after. Men rarely protect and respect the women in their lives. We live in a culture of Abimelechs. The lesson here for the guys is twofold: (1) they are to correct the error of Adam and many other men in the Bible and act as strong leaders and protectors, and (2) they are to value the calling God gives to women. God called Deborah to be a judge and gave her the gift of a prophet. Gideon *needed* her because God had *called* her. God has put women in the lives of men to fill a hole; men should submit to that. Furthermore, men should submit to women when God calls them to a position of leadership over men; it is glorious, not shameful.

For girls, the lesson here is significant. Seize your calling; don't be marginalized just because our culture says you are here for looks. God has given you gifts and has a calling for your life. This calling certainly includes being a Proverbs 31 woman, but may also include higher levels of leadership. (However, never despise roles like mother and sister.) Don't be afraid to live into your calling like Deborah did or to make bold and shrewd decisions like Jael and the unnamed woman did.

ACTIVITIES

1. Compare and Contrast. Proverbs 31:30 says, "Charm is deceptive, and beauty is fleeting; but a woman who fears the LORD is to be praised." Judges says nothing about the appearance of Deborah, Jael, or the unnamed woman; perhaps they were beautiful, but that is not why they were remembered. On the following page, identify things these women did that showed the fear of God and contrast the boldness of the women with Barak and Abimelech. What did these men do that showed that they didn't fear God?

Unit 7: The Judges

How the women of Judges feared the Lord	How Barak and Abimelech *didn't*

2. Gratitude Activity. In the space below, make a list of the women who have had an impact on you. Why did each of these women have an impact on you? _____

_____

_____

_____

_____

_____

_____

_____

Thank God for the women in your life who are bold and fear the Lord. Write a short prayer of thanksgiving in the space below._____

_____

_____

_____

_____

_____

_____

Lesson 7.2

EVALUATION

1. What does the promise in Genesis 3:15 (the seed of a woman will crush the head of the serpent) have to do with the women in this lesson? _____
_____
_____

2. What was Deborah called by God and given the gifts to do? _____
_____
_____

3. What did Barak do that showed his weakness? _____
_____
_____

4. How does Barak's behavior help explain why Deborah was the leader of Israel and not a man? _____
_____
_____

5. What did Barak's weakness cost him? _____
_____
_____

6. Was Jael a murderer or a hero? Why? _____
_____
_____

7. Name some of the evil things Abimelech did. _____
_____
_____

8. Why do you think a woman was the one to drop the upper millstone on the head of Abimelech? ___
_____
_____

Samson and the Philistines

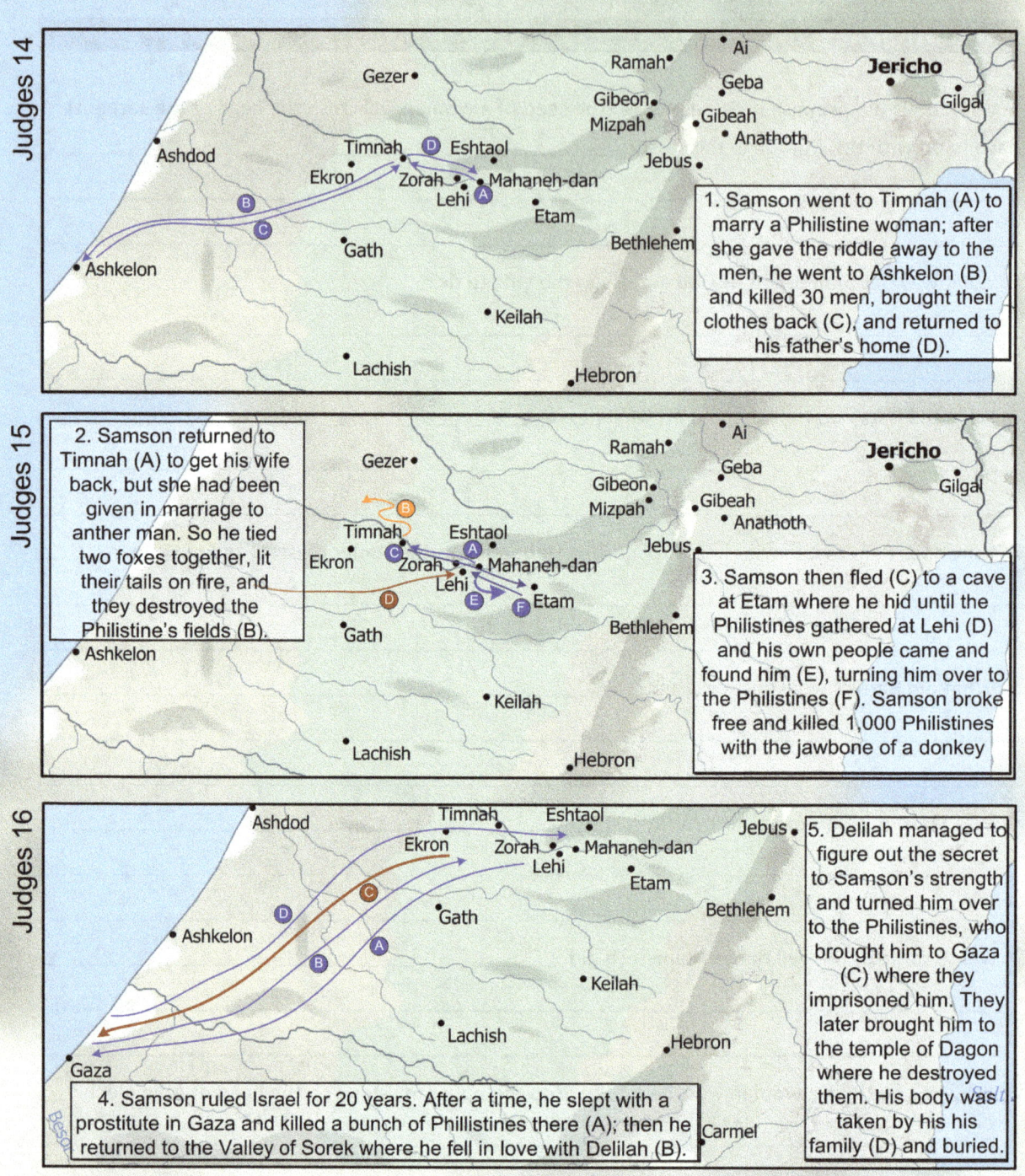

LESSON 7.3

Samson Crushed the Philistine Heads

UNIT 7

THE STORY

Lesson Theme - Samson the head-crusher
In the last lesson we studied the female head-crushers of Judges. In this lesson, we will look at the chief male head-crusher in the book of Judges: Samson. Samson is a larger than life character: a poet, a lover, an incredibly strong man, and a man very adept at creating circumstances that allowed him to kill Philistines. The main point of this lesson is that God, through Samson... and Samson, by following the leading of the Holy Spirit, crushed the heads of the Philistine kings, preparing the Philistines for their defeat.

A little background information is important here. The Philistines were descendants of Mizraim, which means that they were essentially Egyptians (Gen 10:13). When Israel came into the land, they were to completely defeat their enemies. They didn't, and so, as a result, they would occasionally be enslaved by their neighbors. At this point in the Story, Israel was "enslaved" by the Philistines. The Philistines had defeated Israel and made them pay tribute taxes—which meant that a portion of their harvest went straight to the Philistines under threat of another war. Israel was typologically back in slavery in Egypt again and in need of a deliverer.

It is a bit unfortunate how the story of Samson is often told: he was a strong but foolish man whom God used, almost in spite of himself, to bring about the defeat of the Philistines. This version of the story is not quite right. There are two primary narratives that make up the life of

OVERVIEW

Through miraculous births, God gave Israel a judge, Samson, and a prophet, Samuel, at about the same time. They operated in different spheres: Samson on the battlefield and Samuel in the temple, but they both took part in Israel's deliverance from the Philistines. This lesson is about Samson, the crusher of Philistine heads. God had Samson marry a Philistine woman to give him the opportunity to kill a whole bunch of Philistines, including 1,000 men whose heads he crushed with the jawbone of a donkey. But later, things went downhill for Samson; he lusted after Philistine women and ended up giving Delilah the secret to his strength, and she cut his hair. The Philistines gouged out Samson's eyes and put him in prison. He remained imprisoned until the Philistines threw a big party at the temple of Dagon and wanted Samson to entertain them. By then, his hair had grown out, and God gave him his strength back. He knocked down the temple, killing 3,000 Philistines, including their five kings, preparing the way for Israel's later deliverance from Philistine domination.

SOURCE MATERIAL

- Judges 13-16
- 1 Samuel 1:1-2:11
- Numbers 6:1-21
- Proverbs 16:18
- Psalm 59

Unit 7: The Judges

OBJECTIVES

Feel...

- excitement about Samson crushing so many Philistine heads.
- "... really Samson?"—exasperated that Samson faltered and gave up the secret to his strength.
- gratitude that God redeemed Samson's situation and allowed him to destroy the temple of Dagon.
- joy that God defeated His enemies in spite of His people's failures.

Understand...

- the significance of the miraculous births of Samson and Samuel.
- what it meant to be a Nazirite.
- that the Lord led Samson to marry the Philistine woman so that he would have the opportunity to kill so many Philistines.
- that Samson's lusts for Philistine women led to him giving up the secret to his strength.
- how God redeemed Samson's failures and allowed him to bring down the temple of Dagon.

Apply this understanding by...

- being honest and humble about the gifts God has given to you.

Samson. The first one is the story of his marriage to the Philistine woman; the second is the story of Samson sleeping with a Philistine prostitute and falling in love with Delilah. In the first story, it is very clear that everything Samson did was exactly what God wanted him to do, resulting in the crushing of many Philistine heads. In the second story, Samson went rogue and was not walking with the Lord, so he ended up in prison with his eyes gouged out. In the end, Samson was the hero who brought down the temple of Dagon and crushed the heads of all the kings of the Philistines.

Samson (and Samuel) born
This lesson is about Samson, but you should be familiar with Samuel as well; the next lesson (in *The Kingdom of Israel*) will overlap with this one and will look (in part) at Samuel's ministry. Samson and Samuel were both born around the same time, perhaps even in the same year. The Bible records a number of miraculous births, where a barren woman gives birth to a son (a seed). Whenever one of these miraculous births occurred, God was getting ready to do something cool. Both Samson and Samuel were born to women who were unable to have children, double miraculous births, meaning God was getting ready to do something *really* cool. Samson and Samuel were head-crushers, preparing the way for Israel's permanent delivery from Philistine oppression through King David.

The details of these miraculous birth stories are worth reading, but here are the main points: (1) both Samson and Samuel were born around the same time to women who were barren, and (2) both Samson and Samuel were dedicated to the Lord under the Nazirite vow (Samson was clearly a Nazirite for life, while Samuel apparently let his hair grow, but it is not clear that he was following all the requirements of being a full Nazirite). Samson was a head-crushing judge whose work was dedicated to the Lord; Samuel was a prophet given to temple service.

It is important to understand the basics of the Nazirite vow (for details see Num 6:1-21). The

Nazirite vow was normally a temporary vow of dedication to the Lord, and the one making the vow had a task to perform unto the Lord. During their vow, while they completed their task, they were not to cut their hair. Then, to complete their vow time, they would go to the temple and offer certain sacrifices, *including their hair.* That's right, when the task was done, they would offer their work back to God by offering their hair on the altar. Additionally, during the time of their vow, they were to show dedication to the Lord by not drinking any alcohol (wine or beer) or eating any grapes, and they had to stay away from unclean things and dead bodies. Samson was a Nazirite for life, which meant his life was dedicated to the Lord (Judg 13:7).

Samson's marriage to a Philistine woman
At the end of Judges 13, we learn that "the Spirit of the LORD began to move upon [Samson]" (Judg 13:25). The whole convoluted story that follows in Judges 14-15 is all under the direction of the Holy Spirit; Samson was in-tune with God. He went down to Timnah, which at that time was a Philistine town, and found a Philistine woman whom he wanted to marry. The people of Israel were under a command not to marry foreigners who lived in the land because God didn't want them to start worshiping their gods, but Samson's was a special case. Samson didn't want to become a Philistine and worship their gods. He wanted to crush some Philistine heads, and this marriage would provide the occasion for that. Again, the Holy Spirit was leading Samson in this part of the story, and Samson was following Him (at least at this time in his life; see Judg 14:4).

On his way down to Timnah to prepare for the wedding, a lion attacked Samson, and he killed it with his bare hands (Judg 14:6). This story is important because the lion would become an allegory for Samson's interaction with the Philistines. When he went down to Timnah the next time, he came across the lion again; bees had made their home in the lion, and it was filled with honey (Judg 14:8). Samson ate some honey and continued on his way.

At the time of his wedding, Samson was given 30 companions from among the Philistines (sort of like groomsmen). Samson challenged these men to a contest of cleverness and gave them a riddle to solve regarding the lion: "Out of the eater came something to eat; and out of the strong came something sweet" (Judg 14:14). The 30 companions had seven days to answer the riddle, and if they got it, he would give them each a full set of clothing. During that time, they pressured Samson's bride to give them the answer. She finally gave into them, showing that her allegiance was to the Philistines rather than to Samson. When the men gave Samson the answer to the riddle, his response to them was, "If you had not plowed with my heifer, you would not have solved my riddle!" (Judg 14:18), indicating that when his bride gave the men the answer to the riddle, it was tantamount to adultery. The men got the right answer to the riddle, but they didn't really understand it. Samson was the lion; *he* was the strong one, and had they been hungry, he would have given them the sweet word of God; the Philistines could have been saved! Instead, Samson killed 30 men of Ashkelon (one of the five main Philistine cities) and stole the clothing off their dead bodies to fulfill his promise to his 30 companions (Judg 14:19).

Thus began a cascading series of events which allowed Samson to crush a bunch of Philistine heads. As a result of Samson killing these 30 men and leaving town, his wife was given to another man. Later on, Samson returned to spend some time with his wife, only to find that she was with another man (Judg 15:1). When he found out

that she had been given away, he tied the tails of 300 foxes together in pairs, with a torch fastened to each pair, and released them in the Philistine fields, burning up all their grain (Judg 15:4-5). In response, the Philistines prepared for battle against Israel, making Israel mad at Samson. So the men of Israel came to get Samson to turn him over to the Philistines (Samson willingly went along with this). When the Philistines got him, Samson broke the ropes that tied him, found the jawbone of a donkey and killed 1,000 Philistines (Judg 15:15)!

Samson and Delilah
Following the head-crushing of 1,000 Philistines, Samson became judge and ruler over Israel for 20 years (Judg 15:20). Some time later, he went to Gaza (another of the five main Philistine cities) and spent the night with a prostitute. This second story of Samson's life starts much differently than the first one. This time, Samson was not following the Lord; sleeping with a prostitute was a sin. The Lord protected him anyway; the Philistine men surrounded the house to attack Samson, but in the middle of the night, Samson tore down the city gates and left the city (Judg 16:3).

Some time later, he fell in love with another Philistine woman, Delilah. The Lord was not leading Samson this time either; Samson was just following his lusts. The Philistines saw another opportunity to trap Samson; if they could get Delilah to reveal the secret of his strength (just like they had gotten his wife to reveal the answer to his riddle), then they could defeat him once and for all. Samson had proven that he eventually gave into nagging. And sure enough, it took several tries, but Delilah finally coaxed the secret out of him. While he was sleeping, the Philistines cut off Samson's hair, bringing an end to his Nazarite vow, causing the Lord to depart from him and his strength to diminish. Samson's arrogance by this point in the story is evident by how surprised he was that his strength was gone—it is as though he thought his strength was a matter of personal accomplishment rather than a gift from God. His enemies then gouged out his eyes and put him in prison (Judge 16:20-21).

Samson's story ends, however, on a victorious note. One day, the Philistines gathered together at the temple of their main god, Dagon, and had a big party celebrating that they had defeated Israel and captured Samson. The Philistines had five main cities and all five of their kings were there at the temple of Dagon. To celebrate in style, they had Samson come to entertain them, not noticing that his hair had grown back. Samson asked the servant who was guiding him to place him in between the support pillars of the temple. Samson then asked God to give him his strength back and knocked down the pillars, bringing down the whole temple. Three-thousand people died, including the five kings of the Philistines. So in his death, Samson crushed the heads (kings) of the Philistines and killed more Philistines than he had during his whole life (Judg 16:28-30).

Samson's final act greatly weakened the Philistines. Not long after, Samuel led Israel into battle against the Philistines and finally delivered them from Philistine domination. The Philistines were not eradicated from the land; Israel would have continuing battles with them for quite some time. But Samson's heroic act at the temple of Dagon was the beginning of the end of the Philistines.

Additional notes
Normally, the narrative of Samson's marriage is told in such a way that makes Samson look like a bad guy whom God used anyway. We have said

that Samson was following the Lord and wasn't doing anything wrong in the whole marriage narrative. The reason we know that Samson was on the right track is because the passage speaks so much of the Spirit's involvement (the chapter break between 13 and 14 disguises this). In Judges 13:24 we learn that "the Spirit of the LORD began to move upon him at Mahaneh Dan, between Zorah and Eshtaol." This statement leads directly into the story of his marriage in Judges 14. Samson's parents were shocked by Samson's desire to marry a Philistine, but the reason given is "His father and mother did not know that it was from the LORD—that He was seeking an occasion to move against the Philistines. For at that time the Philistines had dominion over Israel" (Judg 14:4). We also have indications that the Spirit was leading Samson in Judges 14:6 and 19. These instances all contrast with the story of Samson and Delilah in Judges 16, where we have no indication of the Spirit's involvement.

APPLICATION

God blessed Samson with super strength. God gives everyone a "superpower;" usually it is not as unusual or powerful as Samson's, but everybody has one. Samson became arrogant with his; he felt invincible—as though his strength was *his* and not a gift from God.

What is your superpower? It may be a spiritual gift or something you are just really good at. Take some time to express your gratitude for the good gifts He has given you.

Psalm 59 is a great example of the right attitude toward strength. The psalmist says, "You are my strength" and gives all the glory back to God (Ps 59:17, NIV). This psalm contrasts with Proverbs 16:18 where it says that pride precedes destruction. Samson's pride led to his downfall in Philistia.

ACTIVITIES

1. Head Count. Read through Judges 14-16 and count the total number of Philistines that Samson killed. Don't include any when a specific number is not given. _____

2. Journal Time: God's Gifts. God has given all of us a "superpower." This may be a spiritual gift or a talent. We don't have the same gift as Samson and probably can't knock down buildings, but it is still important to use and be thankful for the gifts God has given us. Spend some time reflecting about your spiritual gifts using the following question (see next page).

Unit 7: The Judges

What is a spiritual gift or talent that God has given you?

What are some ways you can use this gift to serve God?

It is easy to become arrogant about a gift that God has given us. A good protection against arrogance is thanksgiving. Spend some time writing below, thanking God for the gifts He's given you and confessing any areas of arrogance you might have.

Lesson 7.3

EVALUATION

1. What does it mean in the Bible when God gives a barren woman a child? _____

2. Name two examples in the Bible (not from this lesson) of men who were born miraculously. _____

3. What was the Nazirite vow all about? _____

4. Why did Samson want to marry a Philistine woman? _____

5. Why did things not turn out so well for Samson in the story about him and Delilah? _____

6. What did it mean for Israel when Samson knocked down the temple of Dagon and killed so many Philistines, including their five kings? _____

www.ingramcontent.com/pod-product-compliance
Lightning Source LLC
Chambersburg PA
CBHW081339080526
44588CB00017B/2679